The More You Know

Understanding and Practicing Empathy

Esther Marah

Marah Publishing House

Contents

I dedicate this book to my wonderful parents, K. D.K. and Isatu Marah. Thank you for the love you carry and for showing me how to carry it, too.

Preface

Going into 2022, I wanted the new year to be different. Usually, I would attend crossover service at church and rashly jot down a list of things I wanted to achieve in the new year. But after all the celebration, confetti, and exchanging "Happy New Year" with everyone, the zeal for chasing those goals would slowly drift to the back of my memory like the meal I had for breakfast that morning. But I vowed to do things differently and make it my best year yet! So, a few days into the new year, I planned a retreat for myself, my Bible, my worship playlist, and the Holy Spirit. I had never done a retreat like this before, so I wasn't entirely sure what to do for three days at this Airbnb, but

I knew deep down in my spirit that I would have a memorable encounter with the Holy Spirit.

On the second day, I found myself deep in prayer and meditation, eagerly waiting for a divine revelation in the Airbnb bedroom. I hoped to hear God's voice thundering, assuring me that this year would be one of abundant blessings. I was waiting to see the heavens open up and visions of angels coming down to me with gifts in their hands. But all I got was a few words from a still, small voice saying you will write a book, among other things. I immediately thought, "This must be some little demon passing by sending whispers of confusion" because there's no way God would tell me that.

So, I carried on praying with intensity, trying to rebuke that voice, but it persisted. It sounds funny now, trying to rebuke the Holy Spirit with Himself, but I was convinced I was discerning a lying spirit.

I thank God for His mercy when I reflect on times like these. Because--whew! Had I persisted in my ignorance, I could have pushed the Holy Spirit away because His role as a helper is not forceful.

¹³ When the Spirit of truth comes, he
will guide you into all the truth, for he will
not speak on his own authority, but whatever he hears he will speak, and he will
declare to you the things that are to come.

John 16:13, ESV

Then I stopped to discern the spirit behind the voice, and what I found was the spirit of fear over-shadowing the voice of the Holy Spirit. So, every time I heard "Book," fear rose, and I associated the two. So, I allowed myself some time to wrestle with the emotions I was experiencing and uncover the root cause. At that time, I couldn't imagine taking on such an important project so soon in my life. I felt that given my understanding then, I wasn't an expert in any area where I could write an entire book and teach others. As I write this, it sounds ridiculous because, given how many books exist, not everyone can confidently call themselves an "expert," yet thousands of excellent books have blessed many lives. It was in that moment of vul-nerability before the Lord, and a little back and forth, that He gave me peace and reassured me of His word to never leave my side until He has fulfilled all His promises to me.

> 15 Behold, I am with you and will keep you
> wherever you go, and will bring you back
> to this land; for I will not leave you until I
> have done what I have spoken to you.
>
> Genesis 28:15, NKJV

I came out of that time of prayer still fearful of what was to come. Still, I was assured that no matter the size of this supposed threat, I would not be facing it alone. And indeed, the Lord has been faithful in delivering. Hesitantly, I shared with my spiritual Father, Apostle Emmanuel Adewusi, what the Lord had instructed me to focus on for that year. In that meeting, he confirmed that I would start writing a book, and it would be about empathy.

When I first received the instructions for this book, I wrestled with it for a long time. I thought to myself that this must be a joke. If God were to ask me to write a book, it surely would be about something like wisdom, vision, purpose, or something along those lines so that I could demonstrate the depth of my knowledge.

Oh, how my pride clouded my judgment, bringing along its little vile friends: fear, condemnation, offence, and slumber. My main concern was knowing God wasn't calling me because I was the most qualified or knowledgeable. But through this book, He also wanted to build me up in empathy and reach people through my story. I let out a long sigh at this realization because that meant training was in session.

Proverb 25:2 (NKJV) says, "It is the glory of God to conceal a matter, But the glory of kings is to search out a matter". I believe that empathy is one of such glorious treasures we are meant to discover and unveil in ourselves and for others. As a virtue of love, those who diligently seek to understand and experience it can enjoy its purest form. You must desire and go after it for it to be revealed in your life. And when it does, it will be glorious. I had not even started with the planning stages. Yet, over the next several months, I experienced a flood of attacks aimed at blocking the flow of love in my life.

The enemy was determined to keep me ignorant of my empathetic nature and the well of love God had placed inside of me. Simply put, it was a battle just to accept the vision of this book.

Step one was accepting that God gave me this assignment and, therefore, would give me what to say. However, step two was where training commenced.

As I said before, it is the glory of kings to seek out the hidden treasures of the Lord, which means that certain revelations can only be communicated through lived experience. The Lord had to take me through the rejection, sacrifice, and pain that can be found in love so that I could be refined. I can confidently say that through this journey, my capacity to empathize with others has multiplied beyond what I could have imagined, and I pray this, too, will be your testimony.

Chapter One
What is Empathy

There are some words we hear and use often, like love, trust, fear, and joy. Yet, if someone asked us to define any of these words, most people would struggle to articulate what they mean–despite experiencing them in depth. Empathy is a popular word that I would also add to that category. People use it to describe their emotional state towards another person, but it is much more than what we feel. Empathy is often understood as an appendage to the larger concept of emotional intelligence, also known as emotional quotient (EQ). Our EQ informs multiple aspects of how we use and manage our emotions, including communicating, dealing with stress, and empathizing with people. As this book dives deeper into empathy, every reader will be more confident in their ability to make people feel known just as they wish to feel truly known.

I've always been a person who felt deeply, to the point where I could physically feel the pain someone was going through when they got an injury, or described a painful experience. However, when I received the instruction to write this book, I knew within me that what God wanted to say to people regarding empathy is so much more than just our feelings. As I started my introspection into what empathy means to me, my first stop took me back to my family. I come from a family of ten people. The youngest of five sisters and two brothers, and born to amazing parents, K.D.K and Isatu Marah. People are often shocked when I tell them I'm the last born in my family, but when you come from a family as big as mine, you'll find that you get the title of a last born with zero benefits.

My unique environment pushed me to mature quickly, significantly impacting my ability to remain childlike. One event in particular that shifted the way I approached my relationship with my parents was the moment I started to understand my family's financial position. At that time, I was probably around seven or eight, and before then, my idea of wealth and poverty only existed as polar opposites. I did not understand that poverty and wealth can be measured on a spectrum. It is not just the people sleeping on the side of the streets who could be considered poor, and not only the people who own mansions are considered rich. So, there I was years ago in my childhood home, reflecting on how my immigrant parents were able to provide for all eight of us, and at some point in my time of reflection, I started to recall particular patterns of spending. Things like, how much they had to work and the number of people they were responsible for in my immediate and extended family. With no initial intention of contemplating such a weighty subject, it dawned. "I think my family is really struggling" I said to myself. As the words left my mouth, it felt like I had taken my fist and punched myself in the gut. The revelation I came to was difficult to swallow, yet it opened my eyes to so much truth that I had ignored because of the innocence of my youth. At first, I wasn't even sad because of our proximity to poverty, or the fear of what could happen after a few missed paycheques. I was more concerned with how my parents were existing each day carrying the weight of this information, yet they continued to take care of it.

We lived in a quiet suburban neighbourhood with mostly retired couples and small families. The elementary school my sister and I attended comprised 99.7% white students from middle to upper-class families. With how well my parents provided for me and my siblings, always making sure we had what we needed, I assumed that my family was no different than all the other kids. There are many nuances to consider in this situation, of course, but what this did for me was spotlight my empathy. I demonstrated a deeper understanding by being acutely observant and considering how people processed their experiences. The more you engage with people, the more you know about them. When you know what makes a person smile, or how important their culture is to them, you can use that information to direct the way you interact with them. Those moments allow us to connect with people to make them feel seen. To me, that is the essence of empathy. It is the intentional steps we take to know people. To understand their thoughts, feelings, and experiences in a way that makes them feel seen and nurtures intimacy.

The Merriam-Webster dictionary defines empathy as a noun. It is:

> *"The action of understanding, being aware of, being sensitive to, and vicariously experiencing the feelings, thoughts, and experience of another."*

From this definition, we can simplify that empathy is expanding your understanding to relate with others more deeply. Initially, I found it confusing how the definition describes empathy as an action you take, yet it is listed as a noun. But as I explored the definition further, I realized it's implying that intentionality matters. Empathy requires a person to intentionally put themselves in a state where they can understand or give attention to what others are experiencing. It takes some careful thought and consideration when looking at another person's situation to grasp the thoughts and feelings they may be experiencing. So, where there is a lack of empathy, we can say that the issue lies not in one's ability to care for people but rather in their ability to pay attention and carefully consider the information they are receiving. Ironically, you'll often find that those who describe themselves as "empaths" are often hyper-sensitive and pay attention to every detail. They typically find it easy to read people–not because they necessarily have some prophetic gift, but because they pay attention and take note of the things others just glaze over. However, attention to detail and social curiosity don't have to come naturally to you to be empathetic. These are skills we can intentionally develop as we build our relationships.

It is difficult for people to be intentional about understanding and connecting with people because we exist in an assumption era. Many people have an inward desire to look competent or like they have it all figured out. But when your default is to make assumptions, you leave no room for a connection beyond your superficial ideas of them. My Pastor likes to say, "Assumptions are the lowest form of knowledge." Yes, you can make claims based on assumptions, but then, you have very little reliability.

Take the parable of talents (Matthew 25:14-30, ESV), for instance; a master headed out on his long journey and entrusted his wealth with his three servants, hoping they would care for his property just as he would. However, the first two servants, with whom the master gave larger portions of his possessions, found ways to multiply what they were entrusted and return double portions to their master. Unlike the other two servants, the last servant selfishly assumes that the master is a greedy and hard man, so he does nothing with what the master entrusted to him.

> *24 He also who had received the one talent*
> *came forward, saying, 'Master, I knew you to be*
> *a hard man, reaping where you did not sow,*
> *and gathering where you scattered no seed,25*

> *so I was afraid, and I went and hid your talent*
> *in the ground. Here, you have what is yours.'* [26]
> *But his master answered him, 'You wicked and*
> *slothful servant! You knew that I reap where*
> *I have not sown and gather where I scattered*
> *no seed?*
>
> Matthew 25:24-26, ESV

Out of anger, the master rebukes the servant for his incorrect and self-serving assumptions, and gives the little portion he gave the last servant to the other faithful servant. The servant's mediocre excuse for why he did nothing with the talent that his master left in his possession illustrated his self-centred nature in that he was only going to do as much as was convenient for himself. It also demonstrated the lack of attention he had given to his master's ways and character, which led to him assuming the worst of his master. Part of empathy is being able to understand the things people value, what they believe in, what they worry about, what frustrates them, and what gives them joy. When we give our attention to what matters to other people, we can hold space for them. We can become a place where they feel seen and understood, even if our beliefs are entirely different.

Some people believe that the best approach to life is through an analytical lens. To them, things are dichotomous as their perception of people and things are not very flexible. It is either black or white, good or bad, real or fake. Have you ever heard someone say, "I just state the facts" or "I like to keep it real with people"? We all have encountered a few of those people in our lifetime, or maybe you are that person. These are typically the friends or family members we go to when we want to skip the sugar-coating and shake our brains out of slumber again. Whether you need to find out if you've been wasting your time in that relationship or if the 15 lbs you've put on is as noticeable as you think—these people will hand it to you plainly.

What I find interesting about these kinds of people is that when they make a statement like, "I just like to keep it real, " they have made two incorrect assumptions. The first is that fact and truth are synonymous. The second is that facts outweigh the truth. Yes, if something is a fact, it will also be true, but not everything true will also be a fact. I say this because, from our vantage point, there is only so much information we have access to. Facts are based on the information and knowledge we have access to at any given moment. While what is true exists whether you know it or believe it. For example, take the possibility that people can travel to space. It has always been true, but it only became a fact after it happened and we came to that knowledge. Imagine you are in the middle of a maze, and you've passed a doorway that says "entrance" seven times. So, in frustration, you keep going looking for the exit. From straight on, the fact is that you have gone around in circles, passing by the same door you entered. However, if you were to take a bird's eye view, you would see the bigger picture and notice that there are a total of seven doors that all say "entrance," but only one of them is the real entrance you used into the maze, and the others are exits that have been disguised.

Unlike the person who likes to keep it real and state the facts, an empathetic person will look from a bird's eye to understand the whole picture. When we engage a person with empathy, we consider what is true, not just what is factual. Facts can change, but they don't always provide a holistic perspective on a given situation. Truth, on the other hand, is what we call into play when we want to empathize with people, so we consider information from multiple angles. We think about a person's culture, upbringing, environment, character, personality, past responses, emotions, and so much more. Curating this holistic perspective allows you to see and connect to the spirit and soul of a person.

The late American President Theodore Roosevelt said, "People don't care about how much you know until they know how much you care." You could be the most intelligent and well-articulated person, but if your end goal is connecting with people, it is not your intelligence that will win them over. Your ability to show that you care and want to understand the people you aim to connect with will form the foundation.

So far, I have introduced the emotional and cognitive sides of empathy. However, a major aspect of empathy I will discuss throughout this book is the spiritual side.

Empathy deepens when we acknowledge that we are spiritual beings. Depending on the background you come from, this may be new to you, or it could be something you have heard before. When I say we are spiritual beings, I mean that the essence of our life is spirit; we take physical form in our bodies, and our soul is where our intellect, will, personality, and emotions exist. In Genesis, the Bible describes how God created our body from dust, which He then filled with His breath to give life to our spirit, and our human nature is evidence of our soul.

> *[7]Then the LORD God formed the man of dust from the ground and breathed into his nostrils the breath of life, and the man became a living creature.*
>
> Genesis 2:7, ESV

When we acknowledge our spiritual nature, we can begin to discern how we connect with people beyond what we can consciously see, hear, and feel.

Empathy is Spiritual

When we empathize with others, we usually connect to their heart. That connection we feel is a result of at least two spirits interacting. The Bible explains it this way:

> [11] *For what man knows the things of a man except the spirit of the man which is in him? Even so, no one knows the things of God except the Spirit of God.* [12] *Now we have received, not the spirit of the world, but the Spirit who is from God, that we might know the things that have been freely given to us by God.*
>
> 1 Corinthians 2:11 - 12, NKJV

> [5] *Now hope does not disappoint because the love of God has been poured out in our hearts by the Holy Spirit who was given to us.*
>
> Romans 5:5, NKJV

As believers, we know the heart of the Father when our spirit interacts with the Holy Spirit. In the same way, we can know or experience the heart of another when our spirit interacts with theirs now if you're thinking. "Okay, pause. I thought empathy was just about putting yourself into someone else's shoes to understand what they're going through." Well, yes, but how else can you "put yourself in someone's shoes" without opening up your heart to them? The essence of a person is in the state of their heart.

> *23Keep your heart with all diligence, For out of*
> *it spring the issues of life.*
> Proverbs 4:23, NKJV

So, naturally, what you would feel when around certain people, whether that's love, pain, sorrow, or joy, is a product of the state of their heart. And if you have opened your heart up to them for whatever reason, then you are also susceptible to what comes from them. Empathy means you are joining someone in their mourning, frustration, peace, healing, and rejoicing.

You are stepping away from what you would deem an acceptable response or reaction and not just giving someone room to express themselves but being that room for them to do so. Being empathetic is opening yourself up to relating with another person on their level. This kind of relationship roots itself deep within our hearts, which means there are also certain precautions we should consider that I will discuss later in this book.

Empathy vs. Sympathy

Empathy can be experienced affectively, cognitively, or both. When we discuss empathy, we often refer to affective empathy, which involves the feelings or sensations we experience in response to another's emotions. For example, it's the excitement you feel when a friend shares they've been hired for a new job, or the anxiety you experience as your brother prepares for his wedding day. Cognitive empathy refers to our mental ability to understand the specific thoughts and emotions another person could be experiencing in a given situation. If you have ever watched someone frantically look for their lost wallet, your mind can envision and understand the anxiety they're experiencing, but you don't physically feel those emotions.

Empathy can be applied to negative and positive emotions, whereas sympathy is just an understanding of someone's suffering. Sympathy is limited because it is culturally informed. We usually sympathize with people according to the social. Things that are socially acknowledged as a tragedy—like the death of a loved one, an accident, job loss, etc. With sympathy, what is defined as suffering is interpreted by the person extending sympathy. However, with empathy, we may not naturally understand someone's emotions, but we position ourselves close enough to get a clear sense of their lived experience.

Empathy: Love in Action

Empathy goes beyond sympathy because it's our ability to connect heart-to-heart with people despite being separated by time, distance, parentage, nurturing, and more. Empathy allows us to know one another intimately despite not knowing one another personally.

> [7] Beloved, let us love one another, for love is of God; and everyone who loves is born of God and knows God. [8] He who does not love does not know God, for God is love.
>
> 1 John 4:7 – 8, NKJV

One of the greatest gifts we have is love. God's love for us manifested through Jesus is the ultimate example of how we can be moved to share in the experiences of another. Love is more than just an emotional word to describe our feelings of deep desire, likeness, or closeness. Love is a spiritual key that gives us access to a person's heart. 1 John 4:7

– 8 (NKJV) tells us that to love is to know God. The very nature of God is love, so there is no way around knowing him without walking in love. 1 John 4:12 (NKJV) says that the spirit of God abides in us when we love. To abide means to remain fixed, to dwell, to be present. God's call to abide in Him and He in us is to transform us and make us more like Him.

The more we love Him, the more we know Him, and the more we become like Him.

12No one has seen God at any time. If we love one another, God abides in us, and His love has been perfected in us. 13 By this we know that we abide in Him, and He in us, because He has given us of His Spirit

1 John 4:12 - 13, NKJV

Empathy, our ability to recognize and step into a place of experiencing what another is experiencing, stems from a place of love. Even in our human interactions, this principle is true. The deeper we love a thing, the deeper we know about that thing, and the more we become like that thing. If you think of some of the people you love the most, you'll realize how somehow you know so many intricate details about them. Like their way of indicating that they are doubtful when they raise their eyebrow a certain way. Or, that your friend's way of opening a conversation with several questions suggests that they are preparing to share bad news. We unconsciously recognize and organize several emotional, physical, and spiritual cues when we "abide" in a place of love with another person. So much so that we can even begin to exhibit those same patterns.

Chapter Two
The More You Give

It was a random Wednesday, in the early evening, when I decided to take a quick trip to the Dollarama by my house. I had to pick up new dish scrubs and AAA batteries for my dad, who had just called me moments before, almost like he knew where I was headed. After collecting everything I went to the store for, along with a few extra items, I made my way across the aisle, slightly glancing from the corner of my eye in case I missed something. For a brief moment, I caught the image of an older woman in the corner of my eye, possibly in her mid to late fifties. She was hunched over a large brown box overflowing with packaged food items. I only got a quick look, but it only took that moment for the image of her solemn face to imprint in my memory. She looked exhausted, frail, and entirely out of place as she organized the boxes of food on the shelf. As I watched her, I thought about how she deserved to be taking it slow and not working such a physically strenuous job at her age. In those moments I also thought about other older adults and how they may feel discouraged or disappointed that their youth didn't pay off for them as they expected. In my mind, I kept running into this idea of how I would love to take her and others alike out of this situation.

Then I heard the Holy Spirit say sharply, this is how he will get you. I thought, "Who will get me, and what did I do wrong?" As I tuned into His voice, He explained that my heart was unguarded. I was walking around with an "Open to Care For All" sign on my chest because I was not being vigilant in balancing my caring heart toward people and my capacity to give toward their needs.

Being that I was raised by parents who were always willing to give the clothes off of their backs to the people they cared for, so I was not programmed to do any less. "At what cost," were the words that kept ringing in my head because I was so focused on giving that I didn't think to stop and count how much I had to give. My Pastor, Apostle Emmanuel Adewusi, tells a story of how the Lord corrected him for wanting to be the "do it all" person who meets every need, even when it was leading to burnout. The Holy Spirit said, "If you want to be El Shaddai, you shall die." El Shaddai is one of the Hebrew names of God, translating to "God Almighty" or "All Sufficient One."

It sounds quite extreme, I understand, but the essence was that we could never be all-sufficient in providing for people's needs. Sometimes, we let our hearts take us beyond the limit of what is in our hands, and this is how we find ourselves in precarious situations, emotionally, financially, spiritually, and more. In that Dollarama, the Holy Spirit was trying to warn me of my tendency to be reckless in pursuit of empathy. I believe the cliche goes, "You can't pour from an empty cup." And the path

I was heading down was like a cup pouring out its contents with nothing to replenish it.

It was a surprise to me when I found out a trait like empathy could be detrimental to the individual exercising it. So, to better understand how to operate within this delicate balance of being an empath, I took more time to observe myself and others in situations where empathy was evident.

Empathy is an emotional response that demonstrates a person's emotional intelligence. However, a person's emotional intelligence level also depends on their ability to regulate emotional responses. What I've learned over time is that empathy left unregulated can do more harm than good. For some, that may sound very harsh, and you may think, "We're meant to be free with our emotions, not restrictive." And you are halfway correct. Although, regulation does not mean restriction. In this case, regulation means being focused, intentional, and effective. One small statement by Apostle Emmanuel completely shifted how I handle my emotional life. He said, "Our emotions are meant to help us enjoy life, not to decide life." Essentially, he was saying that our emotions are abundant, beautiful, and intense. Still, they can also be engulfing, unpredictable, and deceptive, which means how we feel cannot determine how we live but can complement our everyday experiences. Aiming to be empathetic without healthy boundaries to regulate the flow of emotions is the surest way to end up burnt out.

As humans, we cannot take on multiple people's full emotions and burdens and still operate normally. With the mix of high and low, angry and distressed, or enthralled and gloomy, there is an emotion overload taking place in one person. Therefore, the balance comes in knowing what to pick up and what to avoid, how to connect empathetically, and how to disconnect to guard your heart. So, how can we do that? That starts with exploring how we use empathy to understand its strengths and limitations better.

Empathy Fuels Creative Solutions

When I think of a problem solver, I envision them as someone who gets things done. That's also my favourite trait in any movie or TV character. It could be the superhero who manages to save the day despite the odds stacked against them, the lawyer who will go to the ends of the earth to vindicate their client or the gentle friend who becomes brave and determined when faced with a threat. These characters' resolve and actions are anchored in the same thing–empathy. It doesn't just stop at compassion for people's hardships but also gives us the power to change their circumstances. Empathy turns us into leaders; it makes us creative and determined, all because we want to solve a problem and bring about positive change.

The story of Jesus feeding the five thousand with fish and bread is a great example of how empathy motivates us to solve problems.

*¹After these things Jesus went over the Sea of
   Galilee, which is the Sea of Tiberias. ² Then
a great multitude followed Him, because they
saw His signs which He performed on those
who were diseased.³ And Jesus went up on the
mountain, and there He sat with His disciples.
  ⁴ Now the Passover, a feast of the Jews, was
near. ⁵ Then Jesus lifted up His eyes, and seeing a great multitude coming toward Him, He
said to Philip, "Where shall we buy bread, that
these may eat?" ⁶ But this He said to test him,
   for He Himself knew what He would do.*

John 6:1 - 6, NKJV

This story tells us a few things about empathy through the life of Jesus. The first thing is that empathy will move you to go above and beyond for those whom God has placed compassion on your heart for.

Jesus was constantly being followed by a multitude of people looking for healing and deliverance miracles. So, Jesus was already prepared to service this crowd of people in that capacity. As He sat atop the mountain with His disciples, John tells us that

Jesus lifted His eyes, and seeing a great multitude coming toward Him, He asked Philip, "Where shall we buy bread that these may eat?" We can translate this to, "Then Jesus lifted up His eyes, and looking at the multitude with great empathy, He said, "I want to solve this problem as well." The original plan was maybe to teach the people and demonstrate healing miracles, which would have been sufficient according to their expectations. However, the multitude moved Jesus' heart so much that a problem most people would have overlooked became a monumental miracle. When we learn to empathize with people, we position ourselves to identify the issues they are facing, and it enables us to take action on their behalf–sometimes beyond what we had planned, or believed we could achieve.

Secondly, empathy will help you be creative in problem-solving. Bringing it back to what I mentioned in the beginning, a problem solver is someone who gets things done, and if I might add, they get it done at all costs (without resorting to illegal activities, of course). That means your heart connection to the issue will determine your determination to bring about change despite your available time, limited resources, or other barriers. Everyone has certain people or specific problems that your heart is connected to. If I were to ask you now what you think can be done about those situations, most likely, multiple solutions would be stirring up in your spirit. That goes to show you the extent to which your creativity can go when it comes to being a problem solver. Let's go back to the problems at hand:

1. **The hungry people had followed Jesus and His disciples from afar.**

2. **The place that they were in was dry, and they needed a place to find food.**

I used to wonder why Jesus didn't decide to send His disciples out onto boats and call forth an abundance of fish as He did with Simon. Then, I realized this was an opportunity to make something out of nothing. Two fish and five loaves of bread became enough to feed over 5,000 people. That's how empathy can move us to solve problems creatively. This understanding has simplified the process of solving all kinds of problems around me. The once insignificant and insufficient tools and supplies in your hands would begin to prove valuable when your heart desires to see a positive outcome in the situation.

There was a time when my friend, a cake artist, asked me to help her at a bridal show she was participating in. After spending all night working hard on her display cakes and treats for the event, she discovered that one of the cakes toppled over in the car on the way to the venue. So, we both looked at the devastated cake and wondered how we could remedy the situation. In my heart, I couldn't accept that she had worked so hard to present her cakes, and it was all for nothing.

Then, suddenly, I remembered that one of the other vendors at the bridal show had a portable steamer to iron out her table linens. If you're wondering how a portable steamer is going to fix a cake, just hold on. Working with a soft and fluffy coat is best to smooth out buttercream on a cake. Since her cake had previously been refrigerated, we needed to find a way to make the buttercream pliable so that she could reshape and smooth out the parts damaged in transport. When the steamer came to mind, I thought, "This has to work." So, we got to work, and I used the steam to soften the buttercream as she remoulded and smoothed pieces of the cake.

In about 20 minutes, what seemed like a disaster turned out to be one of the greatest learning experiences for both of us. Even if this situation didn't turn out as hopeful as it did, the best thing is that I was so moved with compassion that windows of creativity for problem-solving opened up before me, and all I had to do was choose which one to walk through.

A grace for provision is unlocked when we step into love through empathy. That grace for provision manifests as creativity. When I think back to my childhood and all the times my mom would provide meals for my siblings and me, I can see that the creative grace for provision was upon her. We grew up with little money, and sometimes, there was nothing but sticky juice stains and a few random items in the fridge. But to my mom, there was always enough for a meal. She could remix hot dogs, pasta, perogies, tomato sauce, and frozen veggies in 1000 different ways, and it was always something new. The love and care my Mother had for us sustained the creative grace to always find provisions for a meal. The way my parents always managed to transform an unfruitful situation into something bountiful made my impressionable mind think we were set pretty well.

Meanwhile, the financial blessings were nowhere near abundant. It wasn't until later in my life that I realized just how well my parents multiplied a few loaves and fish daily. There is more at play than empathy in the example of my parents. Nevertheless, the principle remains. We all have the capacity to replicate one of Jesus' greatest miracles when we learn to channel one of our greatest human connection tools: empathy. Our problem-solving ability is a function of our creativity, often powered by intense emotions, with love towards others being one of the most pronounced emotions.

Chapter Three
Empathy for Intimacy

Empathy and intimacy are considerably similar concepts. **Intimacy (in.ti.mə.si)** is the experience of having a close relationship with someone else. The word was taken from the Latin word *Intimus*, meaning inner or inmost. As defined earlier, empathy is the ability to mentally place yourself in someone's shoes and share in their emotions or experiences. In an earlier chapter, I shared how one of the driving forces of love is that it leads us to know people at a deeper level, which helps us empathize. The deeper we love, the deeper we can know. However, a key aspect that was not mentioned is that many people are struggling to overcome their fear of intimacy, which is truly just a cover-up for their real fear, vulnerability.

The fear of intimacy is irrational. On one hand, a person may desire to have close relationships with people where they feel seen and heard. Yet, on the other hand, they fear what it could look like if they were to let someone know their innermost thoughts and feelings. This push and pull between wanting to be seen and feeling overexposed stems from a fear of vulnerability. In 2019, the Holy Spirit instructed me to start a podcast. He even gave me a name for the platform, which is highly prophetic, 'Hear Me Out.' At first, I was genuinely excited about diving into this project because, for years, that had been my heart's cry, that I would finally be heard. I thought that maybe if I'm able to share some of the things I've gone through, people will understand me a little better. Maybe then, I won't feel so far away from everyone else; potentially, others have had similar experiences that we can relate to. As I was beaming with excitement, thinking, "Wow, finally, people will hear me out. Finally, I won't be misunderstood," fear slowly crept in. Thoughts of enthusiasm were replaced with fearful ones like, "But now people are going to know all these intimate details about my life, and I don't want people to feel like they know me too well." As you can tell, I needed clarity when deciding what I wanted. In my mind, It was better to maintain a distant, formal approach on the podcast, than for me to get on there and freely talk about all the things I was feeling and struggling with. Being vulnerable felt like I was advertising my weaknesses to the world with no guarantees attached. It's as if I was hosting a podcast called "Hear Me Out," but what I was telling people was, "hear this out", or "hear something out", but you're not gonna hear me from the heart. My style was that I would be honest and truthful when needed but never completely divulge. Be translucent, not transparent. I soon realized that this method was obstructing the flow of every heart-to-heart connection I could have.

As a considerably introverted person who has often lived a private life, I had to contend with the fear in my heart. Otherwise, the struggle to be vulnerable and have intimate relationships would only persist—first, my misconceptions about vulnerability needed to be addressed. I had to unlearn the notion that being vulnerable meant that I was weak. I also had to let go of the idea that you had to look strong, assured, and in control for people to receive you. And the truth is, people already knew what areas I was "weak" in; I just needed to accept that people already knew. When my mindset began to shift, I started to see how much strength was in my ability to be vulnerable and the advantages that came with it. One of the major things

I learned about trust. People are more likely to trust a person they feel they know and can relate with.

> *15For we do not have a high priest who is unable to empathize with our weaknesses, but we have one who has been tempted in every way, just as we are—yet he did not sin.*
>
> Hebrews 4:15, NIV

Jesus, our High Priest, is who he is because He brought himself down to our level. He mad Himself vulnerable so He can share in our pains. When we look to Jesus, we are able to see how God is near to us through Christ. He walked the same earth we walk, made friends and lost friends, received corrections from his parents, had his first day at work as a carpenter, and was tempted in the same manner we are. Before his ministry started, the 30 years of Jesus' life were not just a time of waiting out a clock so that the main action could start. It was real life, like you and I. Every day, He woke up wanting to remain aligned with His Father's will. To ensure He was growing in wisdom, grace, and the knowledge of the word. These things weren't just implanted in Him. He carried grace, yes, but He had to preserve that grace from attacks of the enemy. If Jesus had been unaffected by the things of this world, there would have been no reason for the enemy to tempt Him. He could be made weak because he came in the form of a Man. And that is why he was made our high priest forever.

Knowing that He can empathize with us because He shares in our weaknesses and suffering helps us trust Him. When Jesus says, "I love you, and I am with you." It's not because those are merely nice words, but because he knows what it feels like not to feel loved, and how it feels when those you love have abandoned you. We can draw near to him because He has drawn near to us. Those who desire an intimate relationship with God can do so because Jesus made himself lowly to bridge the Gap. Although I have been a Christian for much of my life, it took me a while to come to the full understanding of Jesus as our High Priest. It has taught me how you can intercede increasingly for the things and people you have made yourself vulnerable to.

The other component of intimacy that I have had to learn is that fear is deceptive. Fear is an illusion. Most people are familiar with the cartoon show Tom and Jerry, which depicts a perpetual battle between Tom, a cat, and Jerry, a small mouse. Given Jerry's size in comparison to Tom, he has to get creative with his battle tactics. In the show, you'll see Jerry manipulate the shadow of a his tiny hands to give the illusion that a large threat is approaching, which then fills Tom with immense fear, and he retreats. Many of the things we've convinced ourselves we're afraid of are due to this illusionary tactic. Being vulnerable is something a child can do with ease, yet we've allowed fear to convince us that it is impossible and dangerous. The plan of "fear" is that you would get trapped ruminating about all the things that could go wrong if you took that chance. Eventually, you would end up trapped or you retreat. Once I realized that the time I spent being afraid was more harmful than doing what I was fearful of, I decided to move anyway. Someone once said, "It is better to do it afraid than to not do anything at all."

Every day, we decide to love, to be vulnerable, to know others, and allow ourselves to be known. There is the risk of rejection and pain, yet we take the risk. There are no guarantees that you will not get hurt while trying to be vulnerable, but the magnitude of that pain cannot be compared to the strength and fulfillment you would enjoy when you nurture that heart-to-heart connection.

Chapter Four
The More The Pressure

One of the difficult lessons I've learned as God has been helping me grow in empathy is that it can be two-fold. There is the side where empathy draws us closer to people in love, empowers us to act, and makes us more emotionally intelligent. However, even when the intentions behind empathy remain genuine, the effect can be contradictory. American psychologist Carl Rogers described the empathetic connection in therapy as becoming aware of a client's "perceptual world and thoroughly at home with it." I'm sure you are familiar with the phrase "walk a mile in their shoes," which refers to experiencing another person's reality to empathize with their pain. The idea of walking in another person's shoes to relate with them better is accurate. Still, the problem lies in our ability to remain aware that we are wearing another person's shoes, or in another person's home. Sometimes, the depths of emotions we experience through empathy can blur the lines between what is ours and what is theirs.

It is difficult to save someone from a burning house when you are both trapped inside. Have you ever seen a movie scene where the protagonist runs into a burning house to help others escape, and then just a few moments after the protagonist goes in, the people they went to help walk out of the burning house? This is what it looks like when you forget the limits of your empathy. You can become trapped in the house when you try to enter the fire with a person instead of helping them calm it from your vantage point. The interesting part many people need to consider is that each person has a set of resources that they can mobilize in a given scenario. In a burning house, they have a clear picture of the layout of the house, including all the possible exits they can take. You may not have those same resources as someone external to their situation. So, when you go in ill-prepared, you risk running into danger. The instruction in Proverbs 4:23 to guard our hearts is not just in response to offence, anger, or pride; it also applies to empathy. Many people claim to be empaths, meaning they are emotionally sensitive or attuned to other people. However, the gift comes with a price.

The worst thing you could do is to become so consumed by another person's pain that you adopt it as your own. Wherein every person you help liberate emotionally, you become the one held captive.

> *Above all else, guard your heart, for*
> *everything you do flows from it.*
> Proverbs 4:23, NIV

You're Not An Empath, You're A People Pleaser

For a long time, I saw empathy as just this noble skill of feeling others' emotions. However, through my exploration, I realized empathy is also about discerning when and how to engage with those emotions. And here's where the challenge lies: how do we remain empathetic without crossing the line into people-pleasing?

Many people, including myself, at one point, often blur the boundaries between being empathetic and being a people pleaser. It's easy to see how it happens—when you're naturally sensitive to others' emotions, you might find yourself constantly bending over backward to ensure others are happy. You begin to anticipate their needs, thinking, "If I just do this for them, they'll like me more," or "I have to make sure they're okay." What's really happening here is that empathy is being misused to serve an underlying need for validation.

People-pleasing is often driven by fear of rejection, being disliked, or facing conflict. It stems from environments where we are conditioned to prioritize others' feelings over our own to avoid negative consequences. Growing up, many of us learned that being "nice" or "agreeable" earned us approval. But here's the truth: niceness is not empathy (It's also not a fruit of the spirit, but that's for another day), and constantly seeking to please others can be harmful, both to ourselves and to those around us. The longer we drag on the facade that we're being empathetic, when the truth is we're not confident enough to say no to people and face confrontation, the more we give room for resentment to take root in our heart. Undetected, people pleasing slowly climbs its vine around each ventricle until it has suffocated its target. "If I don't upset anyone, they will still like me and accept me." That's what we hope for and imagine would happen, but almost never does.

So, how do we strike the balance between empathy and people-pleasing?

It starts with understanding that empathy doesn't mean losing yourself in another person's emotions. Empathy allows us to step into someone else's world, but it doesn't require us to stay there at the expense of our own well-being. We must learn to engage with empathy while maintaining our own boundaries and self-worth. Empathy, like any other emotional state, is a skill that should add richness to our interactions—not control them. And, just like any skill, it can be nurtured and developed.

One of the most memorable revelations I had while writing this book was that many empaths struggle with overthinking. When you're constantly attuned to others' thoughts and feelings, it's easy to lose sight of your own. You find yourself thinking endlessly about how your actions will be perceived and what others might think of you. Almost like you found a pair of x-ray vision glasses, but instead of seeing through a person's flesh to their skeleton, you see and hear what's going on in their thought life. You think you're a master of non-verbal cues, but perhaps you're just afraid. The fear of what they might think and say about you leads you to fill in the gaps with the worst to save yourself the pain of reality. This is where empathy can become dangerous if unchecked. You're no longer just understanding others—you're living in their heads, trying to avoid any conflict or discomfort.

Being an empathetic person requires discernment. You need to ask yourself, "Am I doing this because I genuinely care for this person, or am I afraid of how they will respond if I don't?" True empathy requires self-awareness. It requires us to be clear about our intentions and motivations. Here are some questions you can ask yourself to gauge your intentions:

1. **Do I have the capacity to help them with xyz?**

2. **Am I the best person to help them in this way?**

3. **Can I offer help without compromising my own well-being?**

4. **How will I feel if I say yes/no?**

5. **Am I experiencing fear in this situation? Why?**

6. **Am I doing this for approval, or to make myself look good?**

Empathy is most effective when it's coupled with self-control. You don't have to fix every problem or manage every emotion that others experience. Part of growing in empathy is learning when to step back, when to offer support, and when to give people the space to navigate their own journey. Many people use the term "empath" to explain their emotional sensitivity, or ability to "read" people. But being an empath is not an excuse for being overly emotional, or for constantly bending to others' needs. Instead, it's about understanding people more deeply and interacting with them in a thoughtful, respectful, and balanced way.

In writing this book, I've had to examine my own tendencies and recognize when I was leaning more toward people-pleasing than genuine empathy. It's a delicate balance, but it's possible to be empathetic without compromising your own well-being. True empathy doesn't come with strings attached—it's about offering understanding and support while still maintaining healthy boundaries. Empathy also isn't about losing yourself in someone else's experience. It's about being there, understanding their journey, and standing firm in your identity. And when we approach empathy this way, we can build deeper, more meaningful connections—without falling into the trap of people-pleasing.

Chapter Five
The More You Heal

What is trauma? Trauma can be big "T" or little "t" trauma, but it is an experience that negatively shifts the soul of a person. This means trauma affects your will, mind, emotions, and personality. Trauma to a person's core is like chipping clay from a statue, and it would have differing effects depending on the tool size and the amount of force applied. A big hammer can completely damage a person and alter who they are outright. However, a small one can just make little dents and chips here or there. Slowly, without realizing it, that person is losing pieces of them until they become unrecognizable.

Trauma makes it hard to be empathetic because it skews your perspective of what a healthy emotional response should be. Many people who are traumatized struggle with empathy in two ways:

1. **They act "tough," and believe everyone else should be the same.**

2. **They have a victim mentality, making it hard to hold space and empathize with others.**

These two conditions are also linked to a person having an insecure attachment style. In their caregiving relationship, they likely did not experience or observe much empathy in the form of attention, reassurance, or positive regard. So, as this individual grows up and experiences traumatic events like a health crisis, poverty, career failures, or the death of a loved one, it can be hard to empathize with others because they have not been afforded that same comfort. Trauma will make you feel like you are all you have. It can make you build a framework of "don't be weak" or "no one has it as bad as me," but both are wrong and ineffective.

I used to be in the "don't be weak" category because, in my mind, if no one else was going to make time for my pain, then I probably shouldn't either. After surviving a civil war, immigrating to Canada as refugees, and struggling to make a living, all anyone in my family knew was how to survive. There was no room to be gentle while living through precarious situations. Among other things, growing up in that environment convinced me that if I was affected by the things I was going through, then I just wasn't mentally or emotionally strong enough. Saying this now sounds absurd, but as it was being reflected to me by the adults in my life, it felt like a secure strategy. I don't even need to ask you to imagine what it was preparing my young mind to become. All you have to do is look at how older generations have suffered because of the "be strong" mentality. It wasn't until recent years that I realized how far I had disconnected from myself, leading to me disconnecting from others.

The same consequence applies to people with a victim mentality. They usually display an anxious attachment style stemming from the fear of abandonment. In an attempt to feel secure and loved, they'll make it so the attention always goes back to them. I've especially noticed this trend among a lot of people who have experienced some level of health trauma from dealing with an illness or infirmity. Despite having a strong support system, the lived experience of having an illness can make a person feel isolated and forgotten. People can come to offer their sympathy, but only that person knows the everyday battles they have to fight. When such a perspective becomes your constant frame of mind, empathizing with others can feel like an added burden. It is a strange concept to hear how someone else has experienced pain and measure it against your pain to determine how much care and attention they deserve. It is strange, but it happens more frequently than most people can admit. Maybe you want to ask yourself,

How have my experiences and trauma shaped the way I am able to empathize with people?

It is a challenge to foster healthy relationships and hold space for people when you are traumatized. Even when you think you are showing love and being empathetic, that may not be the other person's experience. A heart that is crowded with fear, discouragement, rejection, and abandonment cannot freely give and receive love. Often, we won't even know that we've been crippled by trauma because we just build systems around our pain that allow us to navigate life just enough. It is like impairing your ability to walk on one leg, and instead of choosing the option of physiotherapy, which is longer but with a better outcome, you decide to remain long-term with a crutch. That's what many of our relationships look like.

Without doing the work to address and resolve trauma, how we relate with people in work, romantic, platonic, and familial capacities will always be restricted. What is especially interesting is that we are not conscious of the systems we've built to protect ourselves from being vulnerable and facing the emotions associated with trauma. For example, many people use the cover of being rational and logical as a way to excuse their lack of empathy. However, being rational is not void of emotion; it means the ability to regulate your emotions skillfully. Shutting down your ability to connect with people and feel emotions is more indicative of emotional immaturity and unresolved trauma than being a logical person.

I didn't know how much trauma had changed who I was until the end of 2022. At first, it was difficult to accept because I thought, "Well, I'm the one who had to go through all of that. I think I would know if it changed who I was." That was just pride speaking. Growing up, I never had the space, time, or guidance to grasp who I was meant to be. After twenty-four years, I accepted that I am gentle and empathetic. It feels weird to write this right now because I had convinced myself I wasn't. Life had convinced me that I couldn't be—even my close friends and family were convinced I was like "impenetrable wall." Yes, people actually said that to my face, and I agreed with them then. Yet, when I started to examine the wall closer, I noticed there were a lot of cracks and inconsistencies which made me wonder. The work of unpacking trauma and chipping away at that impenetrable wall made me feel naked. It is not a glorious process to behold, but I remember God's promise in Isaiah 61:3 (NKJV), which says,

> [3] *To console those who mourn in Zion, **To give them beauty for ashes,** The oil of joy for mourning, The garment of praise for the spirit of heaviness.*

The pain you've experienced is ashes. You cannot give those to another person and expect something fruitful to come out of them. But God gives us the space to trade our ashes for something beautiful. Any trauma I may have experienced may not be my fault, but I am responsible for the actions that come after it. Therefore, I prioritize my healing and restorative process for the sake of the future me and those I do life with. You, can also decide today to say no to a life of stagnation where everyone around you moves forward, yet you're cemented in that moment of trauma.

There are several methods and resources available that help people deal with their trauma, and nearly every one of them starts with recognizing and acknowledging that you have experienced something traumatic. Although this book isn't meant to cover the process of overcoming trauma, as it does require unique attention, I want to offer some direction as you get started. Going to a professional, like a psychologist, counsellor, Pastor, or social worker, is advised, given their competency and objectivity. However, a trusted friend or a capable family member can also offer support to someone working through their trauma. Safety, trust, and competency are the most important factors you want to keep in mind as you search for the right place to receive help. You want to be assured that the person helping you work through such a weighty issue has the mental, spiritual, and emotional capacity to hold space for you. Don't rush past this step; it will lay the foundation for the entire process. Talk to God about it and allow Him to guide you to the appropriate vessel.

As a Man Thinks

You are able to practice empathy when you have a clear conscience. Your consciousness can also be described as the state of your mind that intrudes on your heart. Someone whose heart is tainted by trauma, offence, discouragement, jealousy, or anything negative will have a hard time seeing and empathizing with other people's emotions or experiences. Your perspective of others will always be shaped by how you see yourself and how content you are with your life.

For example, a person with low self-esteem who is struggling to be content with their life and what they have will struggle to empathize with others. For them, comparison will always be on their lips. They are quick to recognize and compare whether someone is doing better or worse than them. It will always be a competition whose situation is worse because they cannot help comparing. This person would most likely have a victim mentality, so everything centers around them. They need everyone's attention and sympathy and can't offer anything to anyone else. If you find it hard to empathize, find out where your perspective is skewed because that might be what's doing more harm than good. The best empathizers are typically people who understand and accept their situation for what it is, either good or bad. They don't project their experiences or feelings onto other people, but they allow those people to also embrace and share their feelings/experiences for what they are. These people are open and receptive, slow to judge but quick to listen.

Chapter Six
Dealing with Difficult People

I've realized that we can only offer others as much empathy as we are willing to show ourselves. Most of what we struggle with when it comes to dealing with 'Difficult people' is understanding why they think the way they think and do the things they do. There is a fragile line between practicing empathy by stepping into another's shoes to understand their experience and needing to agree with a person's rationale before empathizing with them. It's in our nature to fully understand something before we can relate to it or deem it acceptable. But the truth is that when we deal with people, especially those we label as 'difficult,' we will most likely never wholly understand their 'why,' and that should be okay. Everyone has a collage of experiences that form the 'whys' in their life. So, our approach to dealing with difficult people should not be to examine whether their why is valid or not before we try to level with them. Now, back to the first statement I made. With all things being equal, how we treat others and think towards them is a projection of how we treat ourselves and see ourselves. I eventually realized this after years of saying things like, "I hate having to depend on other people to get things done" or "I work better on my own." My impatience towards other people actually stemmed from the impatience that I had towards myself. When I couldn't live up to certain expectations I had of myself, I often let feelings of insecurity develop into annoyance and disappointment, which eventually escalated to negative self-talk.

So, when Mark 12:31 commands us to love our neighbours as we love ourselves, it is not merely an instruction of hope and future actions. It is an instruction that aims to direct our natural human behaviours in the direction of light and fruitfulness. If you are truly self-aware and self-disclosing, you'll realize that you already do love your neighbour the way you love yourself. For some, love may be too precious of a word to use, but how you admire, esteem, respect, or care for others reflects what you do to yourself.

> ³¹ And the second, like *it*, *is* this: 'You
> shall love your neighbor as your-
> self.' There is no other commandment
> greater than these.
>
> Mark 12:31, NKJV

For example, have you ever had a friend come over to your house, and even though you've created a system for the way your house works and things go, they decide to go against the flow? Putting shoes and dishes in the wrong place while failing to ask or observe how you do things. Then, when you ask them why they've done what they did, their response is, "This is how I do it at my house." That person's actions appear so obviously wrong, but the truth is that is how many people's subconscious mind is positioned—driving a lot of questionable behaviour. If I'm used to leaving dirty dishes around my house, there is a large chance I will repeat that behaviour outside of my home. In this case, if I am used to discrediting my efforts after achieving a goal, then there is a large chance I will also discredit another person's efforts.

There is only so much you can pour from a shallow bowl. Or, in other words, you can only love someone else as deeply as you love yourself. If you ever believe that you love someone more than you love yourself, I can almost guarantee you that it's not genuine love.

A few things could be at play here: time and space. Because your interactions with this person are most likely on a schedule, like visiting someone's house once every two weeks, you have enough time to prepare yourself to behave accordingly. You are not thrown into a surprise situation, so, your actions are most likely carefully thought out and planned for successful execution. However, how you behave consistently will show when you don't have the time to prepare or package yourself in a certain way. Over time, you'll realize you no longer have the stamina to keep up the performances, and your natural character and behaviour will be revealed. Just give it time.

The second thing is space. Most of the time, the people we show more love to and are willing to give more of ourselves to are those furthest from us. The celebrities we see on TV and the influential people we develop parasocial relationships with are often the people to whom we give large amounts of shallow love. In these parasocial relationships, we imagine that we know all about this person and have a deep love for them. Space can create an illusion of depth. Because you are not around to experience regular interactions with that person, our minds often fill in the blanks for the information to our pre-made schemas. This distance removes familiarity, which would have allowed the reality of a person's character to settle in. So, when we think we so deeply love someone we don't know in real life, it's because we've created an idea of who that person is for our comfort and imagination.

Suppose you introduce time to the relationship, meaning the frequency of interactions, and space–the intimacy of those interactions, and you still manage to give love to another person consistently; then, you can begin to say the love is genuine.

Growing up, my learned way of dealing with frustration and disappointment caused by others was to withdraw. This is important because lacking empathy doesn't always mean you are harsh, judgemental, or aggressive with people. It can also manifest as being passive and avoidant. Instead of being as open as you can, you would rather stay closed off and accept only what you believe about the situation and them. We all have certain expectations based on what we've been taught or learned through our experiences. Having those expectations and standards is not the problem. How we communicate those expectations and respond to situations when those expectations aren't met will determine if we are well-equipped to deal with difficult people. For instance, I am someone who expects a lot of myself, and I often believe others expect the same of me. When it comes to working on a project or completing a task, I am naturally inclined to put all my effort into it, in order to achieve the best possible outcome. Sometimes, this can cause me to become frustrated or disappointed with myself when I don't meet these expectations. Coming to this realization helped me establish better systems for being patient with myself first and then extending empathy to others. Otherwise, group work could never be my forte because I would be short and demanding of everyone else.

Dealing with difficult people means understanding that, at times, we are also difficult to deal with. Our self-centred nature often makes us believe that everyone's actions are somehow connected to us, and so we take a very personal approach to dealing with others. I think it would help our growth tremendously if we adopt a practice of stepping back and analyzing situations for what they are through an objective lens rather than trying to validate our thoughts and emotions through our lens of fear and insecurities. So, let's start there. The truth is everyone has acquired a crack or two in their "lense" or perspective of people and the world, but the damage is never beyond repair. How you were raised and socialized—which we will get into more detail in a later chapter—will determine how you interact with your environment.

Suppose you grew up in a home with little support, where everyone was expected to fend for themselves. In that case, you may have developed difficulty empathizing with others due to a lack of personal investment in your own life. That is an example of how your environment can make you a difficult person and make it hard for you to work with other difficult people. Such a person probably sees life as each person makes it what they wish because they have been taught to rely only on themselves and were forced to take full accountability for the outcomes of their life. So, looking for their sympathy when a situation in your life goes wrong would be a waste of time.

Now, let's further define what a difficult person looks like. Difficult people share similar character traits. They are typically people who lack self-awareness, avoid accountability, and can sometimes be manipulative. Difficult people don't have a healthy sense of self. They tend only to recognize their accomplishments, which makes them exaggerate their strengths and downplay their weaknesses. This lack of self-awareness can make it hard for a person to learn from their mistakes and grow because, to them, it wasn't really a mistake. How they perceive themselves is often the opposite of how others perceive them. You can usually detect someone who lacks self-awareness by their ability to deflect blame. When they speak to people, they often speak of themselves only in a high manner but also speak to other people in a judgemental and confrontational manner. However, when confronted with their shortcomings, they are quick to deflect and make excuses. If you've ever met someone with a story for every mistake they've made that removes them from the blame, they most likely lack self-awareness.

Many of such people are the way they are because they have been shielded their whole lives. Possibly, their parents and loved ones always validated their feelings and actions without balancing them with loving correction. If they have grown up their whole lives and everything has been sugar-coated for them, then they are likely to run from accountability or correction because it goes against their sense of self. Altogether, it will be hard to have self-awareness if you are never challenged or taught to take accountability. When receiving corrections, learn to separate what people say about your actions from what they say about you. However, this would not be the case if the area of correction is in regards to a person's character, which takes a gentler approach when addressed.

In John chapter 3, Jesus is encountered by a pharisee named Nicodemus, who is an excellent example of a difficult person many of us encounter. Nicodemus was that proud but uninformed friend or co-worker who would try to humiliate you by challenging you to something they know nothing about. He failed to recognize that Jesus was discerning of his proud and manipulative nature. When Nicodemus asked his question, he wanted Jesus to give into his flattery and respond in a way Nicodemus could later weaponize against him. Instead of giving Nicodemus the answer he wanted, Jesus responded with an answer that met a need in Nicodemus' life. Nicodemus was teaching the gospel to others, yet he lacked revelation of the kingdom of God, which would disqualify him from eternal life. In such a situation, many of us would take offence and react in an undignified way that confirms their depiction of us. Yet, if we learn to analyze situations and people carefully, we adjust our expectations and are not so easily triggered by the behaviour of others. Instead, we are able to make more empathetic and informed choices that reflect the genuineness of our hearts.

I use two main principles to guide myself when facing someone difficult. The first one is to focus more on their strengths than their weaknesses. We can even define someone as difficult because all the characteristics that come to your mind when you think of them are negative. That does not necessarily mean the person only has negative traits, but that is what we have primarily focused on and held in our minds. The second principle is to maintain a sense of curiosity about the person you are dealing with. Someone once said to me,

"No one wants to feel like they are so simply understood."

The combination of our genetic makeup and unique experiences that make us who we are cannot be simplified and understood by a few interactions. Curiosity makes room for us to be humans. Every day, we grow by learning and unlearning certain things, so our expectations of people face contention when we only make room for one way of being or doing. I have used these two principles to understand that people can be multiple things. They can be organized and hardworking yet still struggle with jealousy. They might be loving and selfless partners while still grappling with a tendency to overpromise and underdeliver. Learn to take your mind off what you already know is negative about that person and be intentional about identifying their strengths. This in itself is empathy. It will help you achieve a holistic view of the person you are engaging with and allow love to flow unhindered.

Chapter Seven
Raising Empathetic Children

Raising an empathetic child means raising an emotionally intelligent child. We all think we have emotional intelligence until we are met with a situation to exercise that skill and quickly realize we overestimated ourselves. The good news is that we are not entirely to blame for not learning emotional intelligence because even for naturally empathetic people, it takes someone who has matured in emotional intelligence to intentionally teach you. This method of learning is known as socialization. Socialization is the process through which people learn what is and isn't acceptable in society. We learn to make informed decisions based on the knowledge we have at hand and our experiences so that we can effectively navigate various social situations. Socialization works both indirectly and directly through modelling and what you correct or validate.

My family and I immigrated to Canada when I was one year old, and at that age, I was still young enough to pick up any language taught to me quickly. My parents speak their tribal languages, Krio (a broken English from Sierra Leone) and the English they learned in Canada. Also, they spoke French on my dad's side of the family. So, growing up, I had five languages spoken consistently to and around me. Yet, I only grew up to speak and understand one fluently: English. As I grew older and met several first-generation immigrant children who could fluently speak their mother tongue, I began asking my parents why they had never taught me one of their many languages. They answered that we never had time or were also trying to learn a new language (English) to help us adjust to a new life in Canada. So, even though I grew up around my parents, who spoke a different language, I never got to interact with them in a manner that would allow me to speak and understand it for myself.

In the same way, children learn empathy as an offshoot of emotional intelligence through mirroring their parents and actively engaging with the ideas and concepts they are being taught. It is not enough for a parent to understand empathy and practice it here or there. It must be a consistent and intentional practice for it to translate to your children as they grow.

Unless you grew up with parents who were very intentional in teaching you, and English is not the first language in your family, most likely, you are now an adult who struggles to speak or understand your mother tongue. In the same way, it is how we develop emotional regulation skills; it has to be taught to us with intentionality for it to serve its full purpose. You can be around it, and parts will rub off on you, but not every child has the personality or temperament to adopt a skill just by observation easily. It's a starting point; however, it's insufficient to translate such a significant aspect of one's life.

Many times, we are consistent and intentional about the wrong things when raising children. Before you know it, you have "trained" a child to display aggression and run from accountability. Proverbs 22:6 says, "Train up a child in the way he should go..." Psychological research tells us that once a child reaches age 7, they have developed most of their identity, including their personality, temperament, and core values. Unless it is within their God-given temperament, it will be difficult for a child to understand and value empathy within healthy boundaries in their older years. So, what does it look like to intentionally teach a child to be empathetic?

> [6]Train up a child in the way he should go, And when he is old he will not depart from it.
>
> Proverbs 22:6, NKJV

Do As I Do, Not As I Say

Teaching by demonstration means that you first have to practice what you preach. As a parent or guardian, you are a child's primary level of socialization. A majority of what they will understand and believe about the world and themselves stems from what they hear you say and see you do. Strong opinions and little comments shared in passing all play a part in shaping who your child becomes. What a scary concept. The thing with socialization is that it is often hard to trace what influenced what and when if care is not given from an early stage.

For instance, a young man can learn to respect women by the way his Mother and Father speak about other women. Note that children also take into account relationships and proximity. If a young boy were to hear his Father refer to other women as weak, incompetent, and stressed except in regards to his Mother, this could create the idea that it is common to treat women badly except those you have affection for or a special connection with. This is why, as adults, some men discuss women degradingly but still highly regard the women who have played significant roles in their lives.

The best way I've come to understand socialization and teaching by demonstrating is the process of reflection. There's a saying that "we become what we behold," which means the things (i.e. , words, images, songs, ideas) and people we give our attention and open our hearts to are what we begin to resemble. The process of reflection focuses on the role of the person we are beholding. To behold is actively and intentionally observing, looking at, and seeing. It also means to gaze upon and discern. When we behold something, we observe it, captivated by its grace. So, we take our time to understand the details in an attempt to replicate it. The extent we need to behold something or someone depends on the complexity.

If I were to draw a cloud in the sky, it might only require a quick glance to capture the image in my mind and then translate it onto paper. However, if you asked me to draw something more complex, like the New York skyline or a portrait of Morgan Freeman, it would take many days of observing and studying the details for me to reflect a close representation onto paper. That's just a drawing. Now, how much more to become something we're beholding.

In line with raising a child to understand and practice empathy, the role of a parent or guardian is to reflect a clear and simple representation of that child. We often overcomplicate the lessons we want to teach, maybe because it took us several years to learn. So, we think we also have to pass on the information from every experience that led up to that lesson, but that's ineffective. The more you can simplify the understanding you want to pass on, the easier it will be for that child to adopt an empathetic heart posture. Reflecting and demonstrating works as nonverbal communication on the child's subconscious mind.

A person's behaviour provides ample information about their intentions, traits, and feelings. This is important because what we say might change, but how we behave remains consistent until we consciously and intentionally change it. Therefore, what you do to a child and others is critical in formulating their understanding of empathy in interpersonal relationships. We teach children empathy by reflecting a clear and consistent representation of what it means to consider the thoughts, emotions, and experiences of others. This can look like being an attentive listener, speaking gently about people we don't agree with or understand, and asking more than we assume.

Nurturing Vs. Suppressing A Child's Emotions

Many parents will go the length to correct a child for throwing a tantrum, but will not validate that same child's feelings when they've been hurt, overlooked, or are confused.

One day, while at the salon getting my hair braided, I witnessed a misguided interaction between the salon owner and a young girl who was probably around 7 or 8. While working on a client's hair, the owner calls the client's daughter for help by saying, "Little girl." To everyone's surprise, the girl stands tall and replies, "I'm not a little girl. Don't call me a little girl!" Before I could even process what had just happened, almost every adult in the salon suddenly leaped at the girl, shouting how her response was disrespectful, that she "shouldn't speak like that," and that she was, in fact, a "little girl." Initially, the young girl tried to explain her reply, but quickly conceded once she realized her voice was not being heard through all the noise. Possibly feeling defeat and shame, the girl broke down crying and ran to her mom to console her. The interaction was painful to watch, but also nothing I haven't seen or experienced countless times.

Adults are keen on snuffing out bad behaviour with children, but when a child does something admirable, it doesn't receive the same amount of attention. Advocating for herself at that time was very admirable and crucial for the development of her identity and self-esteem. How she delivered her message can be argued, but that shouldn't negate the fact that the young girl has the right to defend herself if what she is being told goes against her self-perception. All I could think at that moment was, "You're losing her," because what that interaction might have done was reinforce the idea that her feelings and voice were not worth being heard. This hinders the child's development of emotional regulation skills and teaches them that empathy and openness aren't always the initial response to others' emotions.

Holding Space

The practice of holding space is essential to empathize with others properly. Holding space means creating an environment (not necessarily physical) where the other person can feel heard and seen without judgment. So, with the story I shared, a better approach would have been to ask the girl to clarify her response and why she felt the way she did. This approach would have softened the girl's heart and provided the opportunity to communicate necessary corrections.

Attachment theorists have also spoken about the significance of holding space in the development of secure or insecure attachment styles between children and caregivers. Many insecurely attached children lack empathy in their interpersonal relationships because, with their caregivers, they were never afforded a space to be heard and process their emotions without judgment. This is why we now find adults who don't know how to be vulnerable, are dismissive of others, or always claim to be the victim. Without empathy, communication between parent and child can become futile. It is like a flow of water being obstructed by stones; the spirit-to-spirit connection cannot easily flow when you neglect to care for your heart. 1 John 4 reminds us of the magnitude of what extending love can afford us.

> *16And so we know and rely on the love God has for us. God is love. Whoever lives in love lives in God, and God in them.*
>
> 1 John 4:16, NKJV

Only through love can we have confidence that the spirit of God is within us and that we are made complete in Him. Children in their adolescence to pre-teen years have not yet learned to communicate as well as most adults can. If they are much younger, they also lack the fine motor skills to say what they are feeling and experiencing. The work of raising emotionally healthy children takes great empathy that is exercised through humility.

I always find it humorous when I hear parents complain that their kids listen to their friends more than they listen to them as parents. Part of me wants to respond, "Well, of course." From a social influence perspective, it appears quite obvious that a child would hold the advice of a friend in higher regard than that of their parent or guardian. This is not due to the child being disrespectful or the parent being incompetent. It is simply because people are naturally drawn to where they feel most seen and accepted. There is a level of similarity, friendship, mutual respect, and empathy among their friends because they know each other closely. In reality, many parents don't know their children and vice versa. The many boundaries of respect, authority, age, and experience can make it difficult for the unintentional parent to connect with their child.

So, when I say it takes great empathy exercised through humility from a parent to raise their child, I mean that the parent will have to be secure enough to make themselves childlike. Imagine how difficult it would be for a child at 4'11" to keep up in a race with an adult male sitting at 6'4". The adult would have to either slow their pace or switch to a slow jog if he intends to stick by the child's side. This is how we hold space for those coming up behind us. This is how we raise empathetic children.

Acknowledgements

To everyone who poured into me so that I could pour into this book, I thank you.

Most importantly, thank you, Jesus, for being the author and finisher of my faith and, quite frankly, the author and finisher of this book.